ABIDING LOVE

BIBLE STUDY FOR WOMEN SERIES (BOOK 1)

Kimberly Taylor

TakeBackYourTemple.com

Cover Image by:

www.iStockphoto.com

Table of Contents

Introduction

I applaud you for deciding to start this 4-week bible study! Each week, you will learn simple principles from the bible that you can apply to your life right now.

But before we begin, I have a confession to make: I have a secret motive in starting the *Bible Study for Women* series. What is the motive?

I want to inspire women everywhere to fall in love with their bibles.

Why am I targeting women? Women have great power to *influence*. With a word, we can inspire others to conquer kingdoms; With a look, we can divert a child from danger.

Jesus said that others would know that we are His disciples by our love (see John 13:35). So I think it is fitting that this bible study series starts with lessons on love. It is called *Abiding Love*. Sounds like a romance novel doesn't it?

When you think about it, that's what the bible is; this Holy Spirit-breathed book documents God's love for His people and His desire to enter into an intimate relationship with them.

When you love others out of the overflow of God's love for you, you can exhort others to live in righteousness through your example.

But one thing can stand in the way of receiving God's love: You must be *convinced* of His love. So many women have doubts about this fact. They believe secretly that God can't love them because of past sins, youthful rejections, abuse (emotional or physical), or other messages that tell them that they aren't good enough.

I've got something shocking to tell you: *You aren't good enough...of yourself*. I'm not good enough, either. Even Jesus Christ himself said, "'Why do you call Me good? No one is good but One, that is, God' (Matthew 19:17)."

Here is the amazing truth - God knows everything about you, flaws, scars, and all. And He loves you anyway!

My Friends, realize that you don't need to be "good enough" to receive God's love! Through Jesus' sacrifice on the cross and your acceptance of Him as your Savior, God sees you through the blood of Jesus.

The bible assures all believers that Jesus Christ, the faithful witness, has "loved us and washed us from our sins in His own blood... (Revelation 1:5)"

Now, because you are reading a bible study, I *assume* that you have already accepted Jesus Christ as your Savior. But you know what they say about *assume*: It makes an [substitute the word "donkey"] out of *you* and *me*!

So if you want to experience God's love personally through a relationship with Jesus Christ or if you accepted him in Word (but not in deed) and need to re-dedicate your life to Christ, then you can learn more here:

http://www.everystudent.com/features/gettingconnected. html

Are you ready to learn more about God's abiding love? In this study, you will learn how God showed His love and faithfulness in the lives of four women: Leah

(Jacob's wife), Mary (the mother of Jesus), and two unnamed women - the woman caught committing adultery, and the woman suffering from uncontrollable bleeding.

Let's get started!

How to Get the Most from this Study

The aim for each study in the *Bible Study for Women* series is to keep it simple. I want the lessons in the bible to change your life. To that end, it should be helpful to know how the lessons are organized and what you need to make the most of your study time.

Within each week's lesson, you will find:

- *Focus Scriptures* to memorize related to the current topic

- *Lesson Insight* that discusses the week's story in depth

- *Speak the WORD* affirmations that confirm your identity in Christ

- *Aim for Change* that provides questions for further reflection and discussion

To start the study, you need to have:

- *A bible:* I recommend the *New King James Version* or the *New American Standard Bible* for readability. I believe that it is important to use a bible translation that you understand for private study.

- *Index cards:* These will come in handy to write focus scriptures on so that you can 'feed' on them throughout the day.

- *A small notebook or journal:* This will enable you to keep track of the blessings/lessons you are learning as a result of this study.

- *A heart and mind that is open to the Holy Spirit's teaching:* One of the Holy Spirit's roles in the believer's life is that of *Teacher* (John 14:26). Invite Him through prayer to show you plainly the lesson God wants to teach you before you begin each study session. Be attentive to the still small voice within that prompts you to take action on the word you are learning about.

- *A commitment and willingness to give yourself grace:* If you find yourself forgetting to study as you planned, don't beat yourself up. Just start your study

where you left off at your next opportunity.
Think "forward motion" and keep going!

7

where you left off at your next opportunity.
Think "forward motion" and keep going!

Week 1: God's Love Redeems Your Past (Adulterous Woman)

> *And we have known and believed the love that God has for us. God is love, and he who abides in love abides in God, and God in him.*

> - 1 John 4:16

LESSON INSIGHT

Back in the 1980's, one of my favorite songs was "I Want to Know What Love Is." One day, I was meditating on the focus scripture and suddenly the old song title transformed into "I Want to Know Who God Is" in my mind.

I believe this statement is the heart's cry of every human being; when we are looking for love, we are really looking for *God*.

Just as in human relationships, a requirement to loving and trusting another is to know their character. One of the ways we can get to know God is to study the scriptures to see what others say about Him, what God says about Himself, and how God demonstrates his character through His actions.

In the scriptures, the apostle John defined God as *love*. Part of love is knowing about a person's past mistakes but being able to accept them and if applicable, forgive them and bring restoration.

A wonderful demonstration of God's capacity for forgiveness of past sins and restoration is found in the story of the woman caught in adultery (see John 8:1-12).

The Pharisees and scribes brought the woman before Jesus as he was teaching in the temple. The men told Jesus that the woman had been caught in the act. They stated that the punishment for such a deed was death according to the Law of Moses. Then they asked the million dollar question: *"But what do you say?"*

Would Jesus join the men in condemning the woman to death? Would He oppose the Law and save the woman?

The men were half right; under the Law, both the woman **and the man** who committed adultery were to be put to death (see Leviticus 20:10-13).

Clearly, the man had been caught in adultery too because the woman wasn't having sex by herself! But the Pharisees and scribes let the man go free and only brought the woman to face Jesus. Scripture says that their motive was to test Him, to have a reason to accuse Him of wrongdoing.

But Jesus did the unexpected; He simply stooped down and wrote on the ground with his finger as though He didn't hear them. The accusers pressed him for an answer; finally Jesus stood up and gave a pointed order: "He who is without sin among you, let him throw a stone at her first."

The accusers were defeated. Convicted by their conscience, they slowly left until only Jesus and the woman remained. When Jesus asked if there was anyone left to condemn her, the woman answered, "No one, Lord."

Jesus then said to her, "Neither do I condemn you; go and sin no more."

Jesus' statement shows that God is about restoration, not condemnation. In addition, He is about *hope*. The woman no longer had to be a slave to her past; she had a chance to move forward into newness of life!

That is the invitation Jesus gives to all those who follow Him. We have a new identity in Him; the woman caught in adultery called him "Lord." We call him "Lord." As such, we acknowledge him as our *Master*, our *Owner*. We recognize His authority to control our lives because He paid for our lives with his own life.

Therefore, we have a responsibility to believe what our Lord says about us, even though our current thoughts and feelings might oppose that. We no longer belong to ourselves. We belong to him.

Satan, our enemy, is called in the bible "the accuser of the brethren (Revelation 12:10)." Realize that this same accuser was there thousands of years ago when the woman was accused. But when you accepted Jesus as your savior, his blood paid for your sin debt. The enemy no longer has the authority to accuse you of anything about your past.

So you can defeat the enemy every time when you affirm your identity in Christ and renew your mind according to what the bible says about you.

God loves you. He loves you so much that he is conforming you into the express image of His son. In him, you no longer have to walk in darkness, but you can choose to walk in his marvelous light.

SPEAK THE WORD

Speak this affirmation out loud as often as possible, based on this week's study:

> "God, You are my Father and I know that You love me. You sent your Son Jesus to die for my sins and to redeem me. I receive your cleansing and forgiveness. Thank you, Father. From this day forward, I live in the light of your love."

AIM FOR CHANGE

Read John 8:1-12 and then answer the following questions.

1. What character traits did Jesus demonstrate in His actions towards the scribes and Pharisees?

2. What character traits did Jesus demonstrate in His actions towards the woman?

3. When the woman was accused, what emotions do you think she experienced?

4. When the accusers left, how do you imagine she felt?

5. What do you think the woman meant when she called Jesus "Lord"?

6. Think about your past. Do you truly believe that your past has been forgiven?

7. If you have difficulty believing that God loves you and has redeemed your past, how can you approach God in prayer to help you with this issue?

Week 2: God's Love Secures Your Present (Leah)

The LORD your God in your midst, The Mighty One, will save; He will rejoice over you with gladness, He will quiet you with His love, He will rejoice over you with singing

- Zephaniah 3:17

LESSON INSIGHT

God has promised to be with you. No matter what the situation is, you can live in confidence that God loves and accepts you. The focus scripture even describes God as rejoicing over you with singing. I can't imagine what God's singing sounds like, but you know it must be awesome!

If you are facing a tough situation and doubt that God's love will help you through it, then consider the story of Leah in the bible (see Genesis 29:15 -35).

Leah was unloved and rejected. However she ended up with a high honor: She was in the lineage of our Savior, Jesus Christ.

But, things in Leah's life didn't start well. The bible describes her as having "delicate eyes." In contrast, it describes her younger sister Rachel as beautiful in form and appearance. When Jacob came on the scene, he instantly fell in love with Rachel. He asked for Rachel's hand in marriage and their father told Jacob that he could have her - if he worked for him for seven years.

When the seven years were complete, Jacob was eager to receive his new bride. But a terrible deception had occurred; Rachel and Leah's father, Laban, switched brides and gave Jacob Leah instead. He told Jacob that he had to take the oldest daughter first. So Jacob had to work another 7 years to get the woman he really wanted.

So where did that leave Leah? Married to a man knowing that he didn't love her.

But God didn't forget Leah; he opened her womb and she conceived sons for Jacob. The names she gave to her first four sons expressed her emotions about her situation:

- Reuben: "See, a Son": With this name, Leah acknowledged that God saw that she was unloved and expressed her longing that Jacob would grow to love her.

- Simeon: "Heard": In this name, Leah affirmed that the Lord heard that she was unloved and gave her another son. Underneath this, Leah still thought that giving Jacob another child would make him love her.

- Levi: "Attached": In this name, she expressed her hope that because she had borne Jacob three sons, he would become attached to her.

- Judah: "Praise": This name shows a turning point in Leah's focus. In this name, Leah declared, "Now I will praise the Lord."

When I read the story of the birth of Leah's first three sons, I realize that even though she was aware of the Lord's presence with her, earning Jacob's love was first in her heart.

However by the time Leah's fourth son, Judah, was born, she focused her heart on praising the Lord. She was grateful for the gift of her son, separate from her husband's reaction.

I think Leah's heart change is one that all women would do well to heed: Ensure that **God is first place is your heart** rather than a husband, children, or anything else. My husband is a mighty man of God; I love and respect him more than anyone on earth.

But I love God more than I love my husband. And the good news is that my husband loves God more than he loves me!

We are content to be *strong seconds* in each other's hearts with God occupying the first position.

I can think of two reasons having this perspective is wise. First, it puts less stress on our relationship because I'm not looking to my husband to meet needs that only God can fulfill. Second, it ensures that we are growing together each marriage year rather than growing apart, which is the danger that many couples face who have been married many years.

We pray together, praise together, worship together, and study the bible together. I believe that, as we grow closer to God, we grow closer to each other.

Wisdom is found in Leah's story for single women as well; single women should keep in mind that God commands men to love their wives as Christ loves the church (Ephesians 5:25). If you are considering marrying a man, then make sure that the man knows Christ and obeys his word.

After all, how can a man love you the way God wants him to love you if he doesn't even know Christ? How can you trust his faithfulness if he is not faithful in following God's word?

Scripture says that if we trust in and acknowledge the Lord, he will direct our paths (see Proverbs 3:5-6). Even if you are in a negative situation, know that God loves you; He sees and hears what you are going through. And as you acknowledge His presence, He will lead you in the way you should go.

Like Leah, you will finish well. Her son of praise, Judah, was the father of the tribe that birthed Jesus. One of the names by which Jesus is called is, "Lion of the Tribe of Judah." You can't finish any better than being connected to Jesus!

Speak the WORD

Speak this affirmation out loud as often as possible, based on this week's study:

> "Lord, thank you that you loved me even when I did not love You. I might feel rejected or unloved at times by man, but you promised to never leave me or forsake me. I know that Your word is true, so I stand on Your word today. I acknowledge and trust you. I am confident that you will direct my path."

Aim For Change

Read Genesis 29:15-35 and then answer the following questions.

1. What clue do you have in the bible that Leah was compared unfavorably with her sister, Rachel?

2. How do you think this comparison affected Leah's view of herself?

3. Leah was married to a man who didn't love her. How did she respond to the situation at first?

4. Did Leah's response change over time? If so, how?

5. Why do think Leah was led to praise?

6. Have you ever felt unloved or rejected? How did you cope?

7. Take a moment to re-read Zephaniah 3:17. If you have ever felt (or feel) unloved or rejected, how does the knowledge that God rejoices over you change your perspective?

Week 3: God's Love Casts Out Fear (Woman with Issue of Blood)

FOCUS SCRIPTURE

There is no fear in love; but perfect love casts out fear, because fear involves torment. But he who fears has not been made perfect in love.

- 1 John 4:18

LESSON INSIGHT

I used to fear a lot of things growing up. Having been a shy child, I was afraid of people. My thoughts were consumed with wondering what they thought of me.

But the closer I grew to God, the less I feared people. It made sense because I learned to develop the fear of the Lord.

Let me explain. Proverbs 9:10 says, "The fear of the LORD is the beginning of wisdom, And the knowledge of the Holy One is understanding." When I read this, I thought "What does 'the fear of the Lord' mean?"

As I often do in my personal bible study when I don't understand a concept, I went to the RayStedman.org site to read the commentary about the scripture. This is what the late Pastor Stedman had to say about what the 'fear of the Lord' means:

> "The 'fear of the Lord' mentioned in the Old Testament isn't a craven sort of fear that God is going to do something to you. There are two kinds of fear. There is the fear that God might hurt us, a fear experienced by those who are trying to run from God. But the fear spoken of here is the fear that we might hurt **him** [emphasis is mine] -- that something we do might offend him or might grieve his loving heart in concern for us. This word 'fear' really means reverence or respect.

> Obviously, if God has all the answers, then the one who has the key to life is the man or woman, boy or girl, who learns early to respect God and believe him and understand that he tells us the truth." (**http://www.raystedman.org/bible-overview/adventuring/proverbs-that-men-may-know-wisdom**)

To me, there is no more important goal that we can have than to attain knowledge, honor, and respect for the God who created us and loves us without limits. We do that by studying about His character and deeds in the bible and then seeing Him actively working in our daily lives.

To see God at work is to first believe that He is with you and wants to work all things together for good for those who are called according to His purpose. How thrilling when you see God's hand at work - when you know it had to be HIM because what you experienced could not have been accomplished any other way.

A wonderful story in the bible illustrates this. Most of us are familiar with the story of the woman with the flow of blood for 12 years (see Mark 5:25-34). The woman had spent all of her money on doctors, but none of them could heal her. Rather, her situation was made worse.

Not only did the situation affect her health and money, but it also affected her relationships. According to Jewish law, a woman with a flow of blood was considered *unclean*, so she likely didn't have many close relationships.

Think about it; wouldn't you be scared if your health was failing, you had no money, or close relationships with people to share your burden?

I know I would be.

But the woman did something bold to change her situation. She went to Jesus for healing. It seems she had nothing more to lose, everything to gain.

According to Luke 6:17-19, Jesus had already healed many people who had come from all Judea, Jerusalem, and surrounding regions. It says the whole multitude sought to touch him, for power went out from him and healed them all.

On the occasion discussed in Mark 5:25-34, the woman had heard about Jesus' power to heal. So she pressed her way through the crowd surrounding him, for she thought, "If only I may touch His clothes, I shall be made well."

When the woman touched Jesus' clothes, power went out from Him and her bleeding dried up immediately. Jesus immediately stopped and asked, "Who touched me?"

The disciples answered logically that the multitude was thronging him, so *many* people were touching him.

But Jesus knew that someone with unusual faith had touched him. He looked around at the crowd to find the person who had it.

The scripture tells us what happened next: "But the woman, fearing and trembling, knowing what had happened to her, came and fell down before Him and told Him the whole truth."

I believe the fear and trembling that the woman experienced was not because she feared that Jesus would punish her for what she did. Rather I think her fear and trembling was out of respect and reverence for what He had *done for her*.

He had given her life back to her. And I am sure she was very grateful.

Jesus responded to her with love and compassion. He called her "Daughter" and said, "...your faith has made you well. Go in peace, and be healed of your affliction."

I think it is interesting that Jesus told her to go in peace. You see, when you have the negative type of fear, you experience torment. According to the Merriam-Webster dictionary, torment means "Cause to experience severe mental or physical suffering."

But from the healed woman's encounter with Jesus, her torment was ended. She could go forward in peace.

So can you. Each day, strive to mediate a few minutes on the sacrifice Jesus made for you. When you meditate on His perfect love, you will be able to cast fear out of your life.

SPEAK THE WORD

Speak this affirmation out loud as often as possible, based on this week's study:

> "Lord, I thank you that your love casts out fear. Each day, I keep my mind stayed on you because I trust in you. I trust you to keep me in peace."

AIM FOR CHANGE

Read Mark 5:25-34 and 1 John 4:18. Then answer the following questions.

1. What losses had the woman suffered as the result of her prolonged bleeding issue?

2. Why did the woman believe that touching Jesus' clothes would make her well?

3. Why did Jesus ask 'Who touched me? Why were the disciples puzzled that he would ask such a question?

4. When the woman came forward, how did she approach Jesus?

5. When Jesus responded to the woman, how did He demonstrate His love and compassion?

6. Why do you think that scripture associates fear with torment in 1 John 4:18?

7. In what areas do you need to experience God's perfect love so that fear can be cast out?

Week 4: God's Love Assures Your Future (Mary)

Focus Scripture

For I know the thoughts that I think toward you, says the LORD, thoughts of peace and not of evil, to give you a future and a hope.

- Jeremiah 29:11

Lesson Insight

In the focus scripture, you learned that God actually thinks about you. Imagine: The Creator of the moon, stars, oceans, and mountains...thinks about **you**.

Not only that, but He thinks so much of you that He wants to give you hope and a future. The Merriam-Webster's dictionary defines *hope* as "A feeling of expectation and desire for a certain thing to happen."

What are the desires of your heart? What are you hoping for?

Chances are, you didn't have an angel appear before you and declare your future to you like one did with Mary, the woman who would become the mother of Jesus.

Luke 1:26-38 recounts how the angel Gabriel appeared before Mary and said to her "Rejoice, highly favored one, the Lord is with you; blessed are you among women!"

In this greeting, Gabriel tells Mary that he's coming with good news and that she has found favor with the Lord. It's important to note that the Lord was with Mary because *Mary was with the Lord*. Her heart was centered on doing those things that were pleasing in His sight.

Like most of us would have been, Mary was troubled by the angel's greeting and wondered what it meant. But Gabriel told her not to be afraid and repeated the fact that she had found favor with the Lord.

He then laid out God's future for her: She would have a son, she was to name Him *Jesus*, He would be great, and be called the *Son of the Highest*.

Wow, what an awesome announcement! But there was one problem.

Mary was a virgin. And like most of us, she wanted details as to how God was going to bring about this future.

The angel told her that it would be accomplished with the help of the Holy Spirit. The Holy Spirit would overshadow her and God's power would bring about the conception. The angel ended his explanation with a wonderful conclusion: "For with God, nothing will be impossible."

Mary's response was amazing: "Behold the maidservant of the Lord! Let it be to me according to your word."

Mary's response shows me three things about her character: First, she humbly declared herself as the Lord's maidservant. She was available for whatever He wanted to do through her.

Second, Mary's confidence in the Lord outweighed any fears she might have about conceiving a child out of wedlock. According to Jewish law, fornication (sex outside of marriage) was punishable by death. So according to natural thinking, Mary was risking her life by agreeing to God's plan. That took courage.

Finally, Mary recognized God's sovereignty in saying, "Let it be to me according to your word." After all, Mary was already engaged to a man named Joseph and I'm sure, like most engaged women, she had a vision of what her married life would be. Starting the marriage already pregnant likely wasn't part of that!

But when the angel showed up and told her about God's plan, she immediately adopted God's plan as *her plan*.

I wonder what would have happened if Mary had expressed doubt that what the angel said could come true or if she had clung to a pre-conceived notion about what her future would be like? I'm convinced that the angel would have moved on to someone else. God's miracle could not have occurred where unbelief was present.

However, God knew before He sent Gabriel where Mary's heart was. He knew that she would accept the hope and the future that He had for her.

Whatever God has given you a desire to do, know that He will see it through. He may give you few details as to how it will happen. After all, if He gave you too many details, you might be tempted to get ahead of Him. Birthing your future not only means taking the appropriate actions, but taking them at the right time.

So keep expecting God to do great things in your life. In the fullness of time, they will come to pass - just as He promised.

Speak the WORD

Speak this affirmation out loud as often as possible, based on this week's study:

> "Lord, I thank you that you have given me hope and a future. As such, I have no reason to fear the future. I focus on enjoying today and abiding in your love, knowing that my future is secure in You."

AIM FOR CHANGE

Read Luke 1:26-38 and then answer the following questions.

1. When the angel appeared before Mary, how did He greet her?

2. Why did think he needed to tell her not to be afraid?

3. What vision of the future did the angel give to Mary?

4. What was Mary's first response?

5. After Mary received more information, what was her final response?

6. What do you think could have kept the vision from coming to pass in Mary's life?

7. Has God given you a vision of your future? Do you believe it can come to pass? If not, ask God in prayer to help you with your unbelief.

Study Summary

In the *Abiding Love* bible study, you discovered that the bible documents God's love for His people and His desire to enter into an intimate relationship with them.

You learned how God showed His love and faithfulness in the lives of four women: Leah (Jacob's wife), Mary (the mother of Jesus), and two unnamed women - the woman caught committing adultery, and the woman suffering from uncontrollable bleeding.

When you believe in God's love for you, you can love others out of the overflow and exhort them to live in righteousness through your example.

POINTS TO REMEMBER

- God is about restoration, not condemnation. He forgives our sins as we confess them and gives us hope. We no longer have to be a slave to our pasts; in Jesus, we can move forward into newness of life!

- Ensure that God is first place is your heart rather than a husband, children, or anything else. Praise the Lord often and you will experience His presence in your present situation.

- Each day, strive to mediate a few minutes on the sacrifice Jesus made for you. When you meditate on His perfect love, you will be able to cast fear out of your life.

- God has promised to give you a hope and a future. So keep expecting God to do great things in your life. In the fullness of time, they will come to pass - just as He promised.

About the Author

"Just wanted to again thank you for sharing your unique and engaging presentation to help us take back our temples! You were truly a blessing and I know that many were enlightened by what you shared."

- **Danese Turner, Turner Chapel AME, Marietta GA**

Kimberly Taylor is the creator of **Takebackyourtemple.com**, a website that inspires Christians to Spiritual, emotional, and physical health. She is the author of the ebook *Take Back Your Temple* and the books ***The Weight Loss Scriptures***, ***God's Word is Food***, and **many others**.

Once 240 pounds and a size 22, Kim lost 85 pounds through renewing her mind and taking action upon God's word. Her experience led her to establish the **Take Back Your Temple** website. "Take Back Your Temple" is a prayer that asks God to take control of your body and your life so He can use them for His purpose and agenda.

Kim's weight loss success story has been featured on CBN's *The 700 Club,* and in *Prevention Magazine, Essence Magazine, Charisma Magazine* and many other magazines and newspapers. She has also been interviewed on various radio programs.

Kim exhorts people of faith to become good stewards of all the resources God has given to them, including time, money, talents, and physical health. "I am passionate about empowering others to adopt healthy lifestyles so they can fulfill their God-given purpose," she says.

"My dream is for God's people to stand apart because we are healthy, prosperous and living the abundant life to which we are called. I want non-believers to look at us and want what we have: Spiritual, mental, and physical wholeness. Then when they ask us what we are doing differently, we can tell them about Jesus, the author and finisher of our faith."

Stay Connected

You can stay connected with Kimberly Taylor through the following channels:

Amazon Author Page

You can learn about all of Kimberly Taylor's books and eBooks available on Amazon.com at one convenient location: **https://www.amazon.com/author/kimberlyytaylor**

Take Back Your Temple website

Kimberly's website, **www.takebackyourtemple.com/** shares her testimony of deliverance from emotional overeating through the change God made in her heart and mind. Hundreds of free articles on the website encourage other Christians on the road to Spiritual, emotional, and physical health.

Facebook

You can connect with Kimberly on Facebook at **http://www.facebook.com/takebackyourtemple**. She also moderates a secret Facebook support group comprised of believers who struggle with emotional eating and are working to change their health. Details on how to join the group are available at *takebackyourtemple.com*.

Twitter

Follow Kimberly on Twitter at **twitter.com/tbytkimberly**

Pinterest

You can view Kim's Pinterest boards at **http://pinterest.com/tbyt/**

www.ingramcontent.com/pod-product-compliance
Lightning Source LLC
Chambersburg PA
CBHW060629030426
42337CB00018B/3270